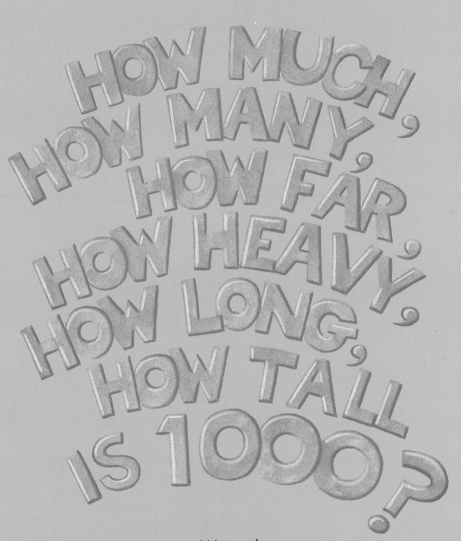

HOW MUCH, HOW MANY, HOW FAR, HOW HEAVY, HOW LONG, HOW TALL IS 1000?

Written by
HELEN NOLAN

Illustrated by
TRACY WALKER

Kids Can Press

For my parents, a thousand thanks for your love and support — T.W.

Text © 1995 Helen Nolan
Illustrations © 1995 Tracy Walker

Kids Can Press acknowledges the financial support of the Ontario Arts Council,
the Canada Council for the Arts and the Government of Canada, through the CBF, for our publishing activity.

Published in Canada by
Kids Can Press Ltd.
25 Dockside Drive
Toronto, ON M5A 0B5

Published in the U.S. by
Kids Can Press Ltd.
2250 Military Road
Tonawanda, NY 14150

www.kidscanpress.com

The artwork in this book was rendered in watercolour and pencil crayon.

The hardcover edition of this book is smyth sewn casebound.
The paperback edition of this book is limp sewn with a drawn-on cover.
Manufactured in Buji, Shenzhen, China, in 6/2014 by WKT Company

CM 95 0 9 8 7 6 5 4 3
CM PA 01 15 14 13 12 11

Library and Archives Canada Cataloguing in Publication

Nolan, Helen, 1930–

How much, how many, how far, how heavy, how long, how tall is 1000?

ISBN 978-1-55074-164-3 (bound) ISBN 978-1-55074-816-1 (pbk.)

1. Thousand (The number) — Juvenile literature.
I. Walker, Tracy. II. Title.

QA141.3.N63 1995   j513.5'5   C95-930522-X

Kids Can Press is a corus™ Entertainment company

How much, how many, how far, how heavy, how long, how tall is 1000?

On a warm day, a hillside is often sprinkled with yellow dandelions. Could there be 1000? What does 1000 look like?

If you collect 1000 acorns and put them in a pile,
the pile won't be very big.

But if the 1000 acorns grow into oak trees,
they'll make a whole forest.

1000 sheets of paper neatly stacked
make a pile about as high as four thick books.

But if the wind blows the paper around,
1000 sheets will litter an entire neighbourhood.

1000 people sitting in rows will fill a small hockey arena.

But if the 1000 people are all waiting to get in,
the line they make will stretch out the door,
down the street and right around the block.

How much is 1000? Is it a lot?

That depends. If you don't like freckles, 1000 of them is a lot.

But when it comes to hair, 1000 isn't very many.

1000 bricks seem like a lot.
Could you build a house with them?

1000 bricks would only make a teeny-tiny house,
with one very small room.
Would this be enough space for you?

What about 1000 french fries? Could you eat all of them?

Even if you *loved* fries, 1000 would be too much for one person.
You could share them. A single serving has about 40 fries.
How many friends would 1000 french fries feed?

How much space do 1000 pennies take up?
Could you put them in your pocket?

Probably not, even if your pocket is quite big.
Even if you used two pockets.
Maybe if you used *all* your pockets.

How far is 1000 steps?
Would you be tired if you walked that far?

If you walked the bases on a regular baseball diamond, 1000 steps would take you around about four times. But if you ran, 1000 steps would take you around about ten times. Would that make you tired?

How tall is a stack of 1000 pennies? Is it as tall as you are?

A stack of 1000 pennies is about as tall as an eleven-year-old, but a stack of 1000 dimes would be about as tall as a seven-year-old.

How heavy are 1000 cookies? Could you lift them?

If you can lift a two-year-old, you could lift 1000 Oreo cookies. But 1000 large oatmeal-raisin cookies could be as heavy as an eight-year-old.

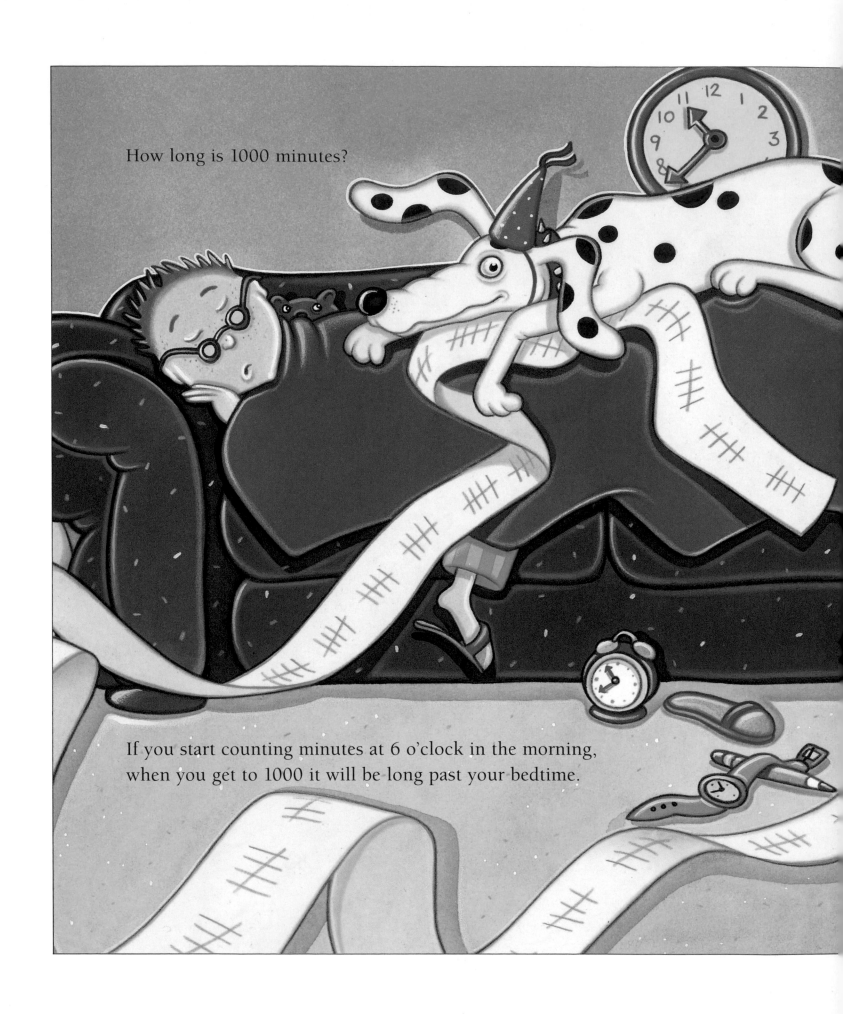

How long is 1000 minutes?

If you start counting minutes at 6 o'clock in the morning, when you get to 1000 it will be long past your bedtime.

How long is 1000 days?

If today were your seventh birthday,
in 1000 days you would be almost 10 years old.

Sometimes 1000 doesn't seem like very much at all.
But sometimes it seems like a great many.

So, now that you know how much 1000 is,
what do you think a thousand 1000s would be?

(It's a million.)

Note to Parents

How long would it take to count to 1000 one by one? Probably too long for you to bother! As children learn about ever larger numbers, counting becomes less practical, but understanding those numbers becomes more and more important.

One good way for your child to learn about large numbers is to do a lot of estimating. There are many everyday opportunities to do this. You can guess the number of building blocks in a structure, straws in a box, or people in a crowd. Make estimating a game you play together. At bath time, estimate how many tiles there are in the bathroom. When grocery shopping, estimate the number of beans in a bag. At home, estimate how many items your child has in a collection of hockey cards, coins or stickers.

Another way to learn about large numbers is to count things by grouping them. First make groups of 10 and then count by 10s to make a pile of 100. Make more piles of 100 and then count by 100s to 1000. You do this, not just because it makes counting easier,

but because our number system is based on 10s: 10 ones make a ten, 10 tens make a hundred, and 10 hundreds make a thousand. This system becomes real to children only through many hands-on experiences. You can use macaroni, dried beans, cereal O's, pennies, beads or nuts to count to 1000. You can also use gift wrap or wallpaper that has small figures on it, circling the groups with crayons.

You can use other groupings, such as 20s or 25s, to make groups of 100. For example, you can make a row of 25 asterisks on a computer. Copy the 25 asterisks until you have 100. Copy the 100 asterisks until you have 1000. Print them out.

Numbers are all around you. Have fun exploring them with your child.